Farms

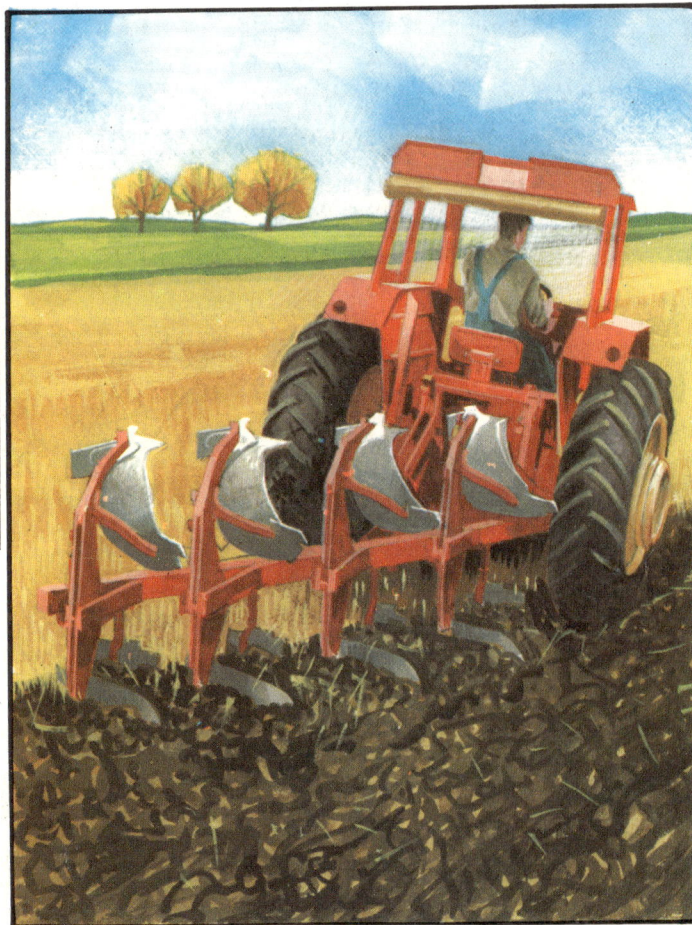

Macdonald Educational

Life on a Farm

How would you like to be a gardener, a mechanic, a midwife, a scientist, a weather forecaster and a businessman? You may have to do all these things if you are a farmer. The farmer's job is to produce food. They may grow crops, such as wheat, potatoes, vegetables or fruit, for people to eat. Or they may grow cereals, root crops or grass which can be fed to livestock. These farm animals convert the crops into food for people. Poultry give us eggs, cows give milk. Most farm animals provide us with meat when they are slaughtered.

Some farmers manage mixed farms where they have several kinds of animals and grow crops as well. But many farmers raise just one kind of crop or animal, choosing one which grows well on their land. Rich grassy meadows by a river may be too wet for growing crops but are ideal for grazing dairy cattle. Hills that are too steep and stony to plough may be good grazing for sheep.

The weather is important to the farmer because crops need the right amount of sun and rain to make them grow. Most animals need protecting in bad weather. Many animals are now reared in special buildings. Automatic machinery can be used to give them the right amounts of food, water and light. Animals such as geese and goats are not often kept now because it is difficult to rear them in large numbers using these modern methods.

Nowadays machines do most of the heavy work on farms. Tractors replaced horses long ago. Donkeys are no longer needed to pull carts. One combine harvester can do the work of many people. Today, the machine workshop is often the busiest place on a farm.

Farm and Farm Animals

You will need

large sheet of wood or strong cardboard · plastic bottles · cardboard boxes · sweet tube · thin card · tracing paper · spills · pencil · scissors · sticky tape · paints · brush · glue · cotton · pins · straws · pipe cleaners

1. Start building your farm on a large piece of wood or cardboard. Paint a box to look like a farmhouse. Use the lid, flaps and an extra piece to make the roof.

2. Make barns and outbuildings from boxes and card. Corrugated paper will look very realistic on the roofs.

3. Plastic bottles make tower silos for storing grain on this modern farm.

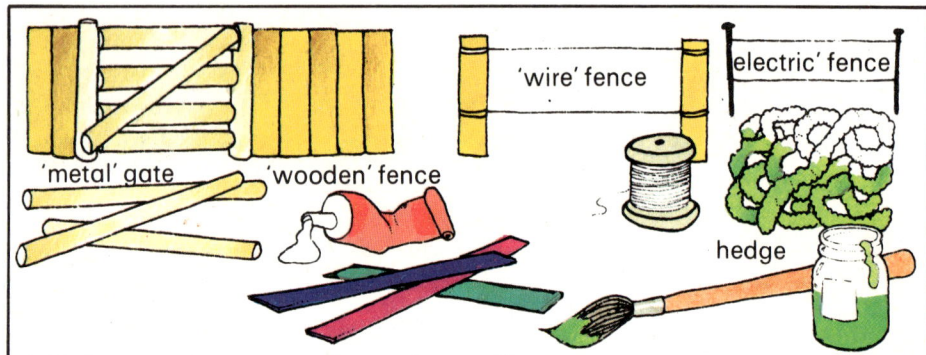

4. Make gates from straws, fences from spills, cotton and pins, and hedges from painted pipe cleaners.

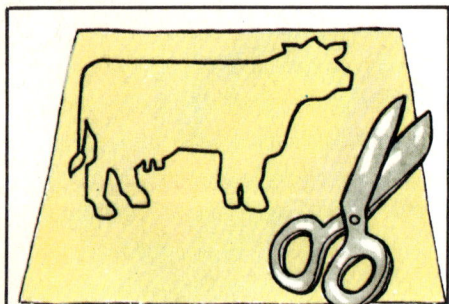

'metal' gate · 'wooden' fence · 'wire' fence · 'electric' fence · hedge

5. Draw the outlines of different animals on card. Cut them out and paint them.

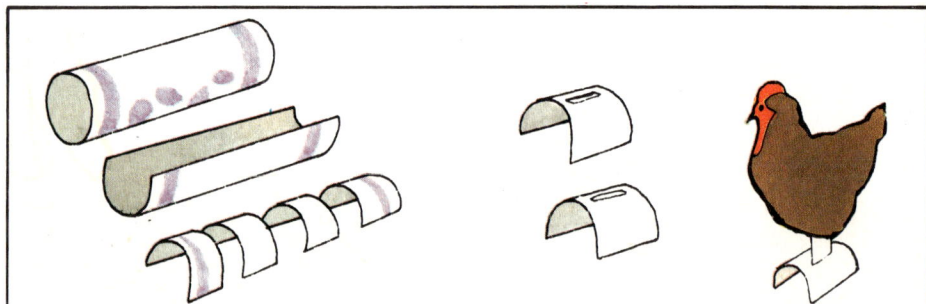

6. To make the animals stand up, cut a sweet tube in half lengthwise, cut it into curved strips and cut a slot in each strip. Push the animals' legs into the slot.

Here are some animal shapes for you to trace if you want.

Paint fields, paths and roads around the farm. Use different colours for different crops. Paint in a pond.

You could give your animals real coats. Snipped up bits of pipe cleaner can be glued onto sheep. Make a mane and a tail for the horse from cotton.

Cattle

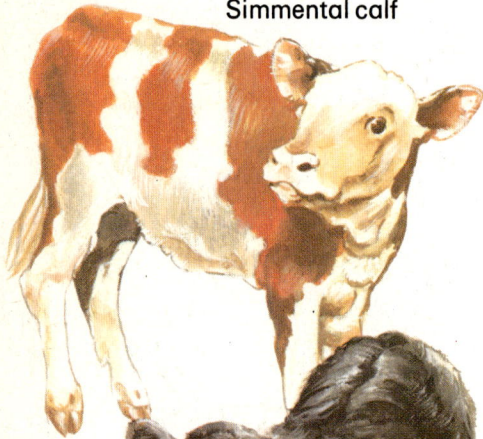

Simmental calf

Angus calf

Jersey calf

The beef cattle which graze on the vast, grassy plains in North and South America and Australia provide meat for millions of people. Some beef cattle are fattened up quickly in covered yards where they are fed mostly on barley to produce barley beef. The meat from calves is called veal.

Beef cows have hardly any milk but dairy cows give about 4000 litres of milk a year. They feed on lush grassland in rainy countries such as Britain and New Zealand.

Cows have to be milked twice a day. In a modern milking parlour this is done quickly and cleanly by machinery. Rubber cups are attached to the cows' teats. They squeeze the teats and the milk flows from the udder, down a pipe into a measuring jar, and then into a cooled storage tank. It is kept there until it is collected by a large tanker and taken to the dairy where it is put into bottles. Some milk is processed to make butter, cheese, cream and dried milk.

Friesian cows give the most milk. Jersey cows give less milk but it is more creamy. Dairy Shorthorn and Red-and-White are both dual-purpose breeds which give plenty of milk and a lot of meat.

Manure is another useful product that comes from cattle. It is made from the animals' droppings mixed with straw. It is spread on the fields to help the crops to grow. These crops may include grass and barley which will be fed to yet more cattle.

When cattle are slaughtered, no part is wasted. The hides are tanned to make leather. The hooves, horns and bones are crushed and made into glue or fertiliser. The blood is dried and made into fertiliser too.

Red-and-white cow
(dual-purpose breed)

Ayrshire cow
(dairy breed)

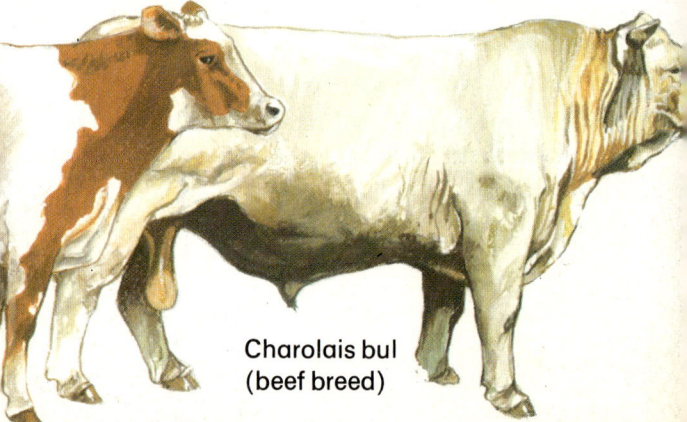

Charolais bul
(beef breed)

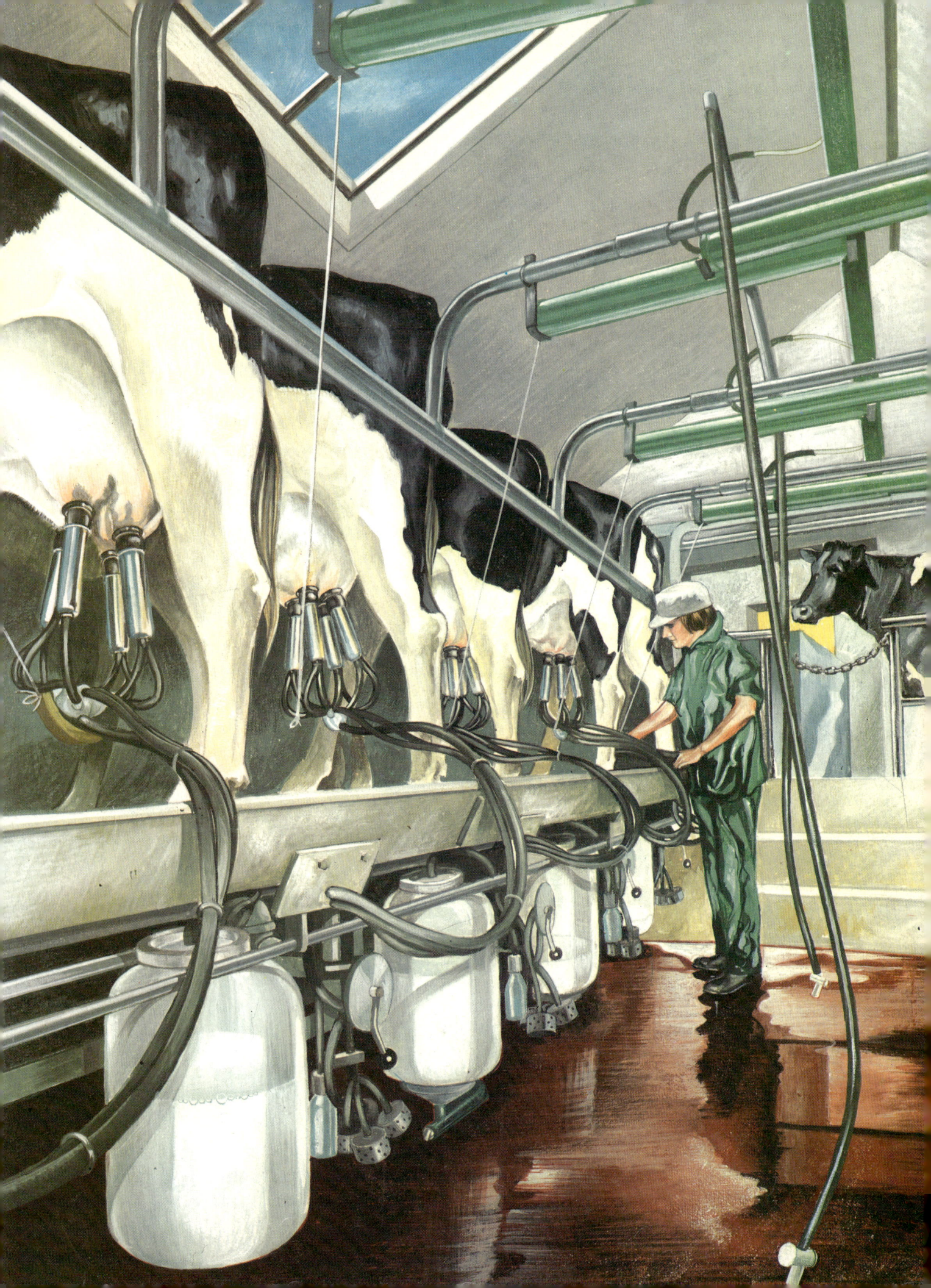

Milking Time

by Elizabeth Madox Roberts

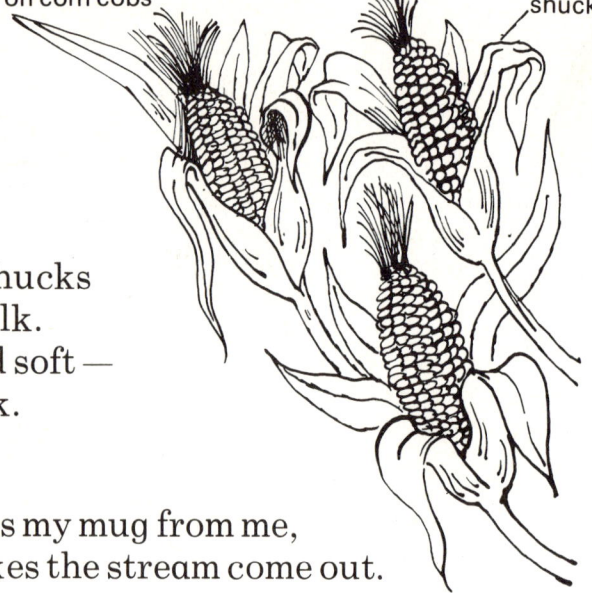

Shucks are the leaves
on corn cobs

silk

shucks

When supper time is almost come,
But not quite here, I cannot wait,
And so I take my china mug
And go down by the milking gate.

The cow is always eating shucks
And spilling off the little silk.
Her purple eyes are big and soft —
She always smells like milk.

And Father takes my mug from me,
And then he makes the stream come out.
I see it going in my mug
And foaming all about.

And when it's piling very high,
And when some little streams commence
To run and drip along the sides,
He hands it to me through the fence.

Who Grows What?

Tom, Tim, Jan, Jim, John and Dan are all farmers. Each of them grows a different type of crop or rears one kind of animal. Can you find your way through the country lanes to find out who grows, or rears, what? You must keep to the roads and you should not climb over walls or open gates.

Jan

Jim

Tom

Tim

John

Dan

11

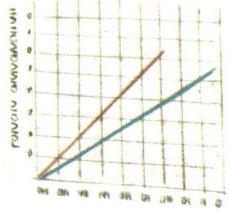

farrowing pen

heater

feed hopper

Pigs

Pigs are reared to give us pork or bacon. Some farmers keep female pigs, or sows, and breed piglets from them. A sow can have over twenty piglets a year. Farmers with fattening houses buy some of the piglets and fatten them up quickly.

When a sow is ready to give birth to a litter of piglets, she is put into a **farrowing pen.** The narrow metal fences prevent her from rolling onto her piglets while they feed from her. The piglets cannot snuggle round her so a heating lamp is used to keep them warm until they are about three weeks old. When they are big enough, the piglets are weaned by giving them food to eat from a container instead of letting them drink only sow's milk. They learn to eat from a **feed hopper.** This food container allows pig meal to trickle steadily into a trough so that the pigs have as much food as they want. They grow very quickly because they eat so much. They help themselves to water by pressing their noses on a valve.

'Porkers' that have been fed on very fattening food are slaughtered when they are about three months old. 'Baconers' are kept for about another two months, until they are nearly twice the size of a porker.

Pigs are intelligent animals. They are very clean and will only use one part of their pen as a lavatory. They can be very troublesome if they get bored or bad-tempered. Tail-biting is one bad habit farmers have to watch out for. They are also quite delicate animals and can catch colds or sun-stroke if they are not protected from the weather. Most modern piggeries are completely under cover.

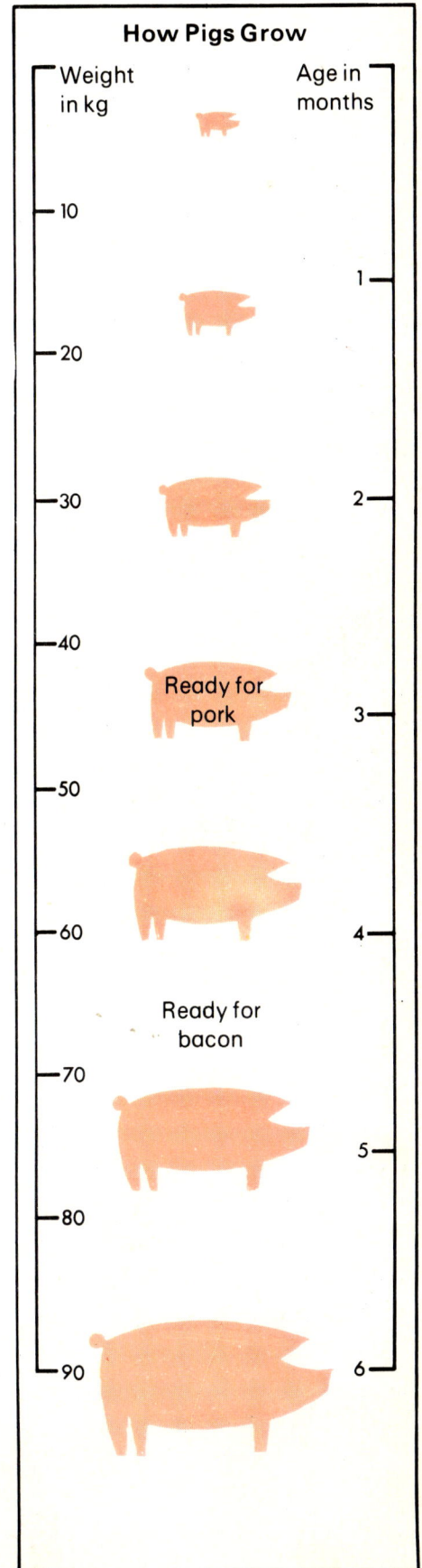

How Pigs Grow

Weight in kg	Age in months
10	
20	1
30	2
40	
Ready for pork	3
50	
60	4
Ready for bacon	
70	5
80	
90	6

Moses the Kitten

by James Herriot

It was going to take a definite effort of will to get out of the car. The wind almost tore the handle from my fingers as I got out but I managed to crash the door shut before stumbling over the frozen mud to the gate. Muffled as I was in heavy coat and scarf pulled up to my ears I could feel the icy gusts biting at my face, whipping up my nose and hammering painfully into the air spaces in my head.

I had driven through and, streaming-eyed, was about to get back into the car when I noticed something unusual. There was a frozen pond just off the path and among the rime-covered rushes which fringed the surface a small object stood out, shiny black.

I went over and looked closer. It was a tiny kitten, probably about six weeks old, huddled and immobile, eyes tightly closed. Bending down, I poked gently at the furry body. It must be dead; a morsel like this couldn't possibly survive in such cold . . . but no, there was a spark of life because the mouth opened soundlessly for a second then closed.

Quickly I lifted the little creature and tucked it inside my coat. As I drove into the farmyard I called to the farmer who was carrying two buckets out of the calf house. 'I've got one of your kittens here, Mr Butler. It must have strayed outside.'

Mr Butler put down his buckets and looked blank. 'Kitten? We haven't got no kittens at present'.

'Well he must have come from somewhere else,' I said. 'Though I can't imagine anything so small travelling very far. It's rather mysterious'.

I held the kitten out and he engulfed it with his big, work-roughened hand.

'Poor little begger, he's only just alive. I'll take him into t'house and see if the missus can do owt for him'.

In the farm kitchen Mrs Butler was all concern. 'Oh what a shame!' She smoothed back the bedraggled hair with one finger. 'And it's got such a pretty face'. She looked up at me. 'What is it, anyway, a him or a her?'

I took a quick look behind the hind legs. 'It's a Tom'.

'Right,' she said. 'I'll get some warm milk into him but first of all we'll give him the old cure'.

She went over to the fireside oven on the big black kitchen range, opened the door and popped him inside.

I smiled. It was the classical procedure when new-born lambs were found suffering from cold and exposure; into the oven they went and the results were often dramatic. Mrs Butler left the door partly open and I could just see the little black figure inside; he didn't seem to care much what was happening to him.

The next hour I spent in the byre wrestling with the hind feet of a cow. By the time I had finished the sweat was running into my eyes and I had quite forgotten the cold day outside.

Still, I thought, as I eased the kinks from my spine when I had finished, there were compensations. There was a satisfaction in the sight of the cow standing comfortably on two almost normal looking feet.

'Well that's summat like,' Mr Butler grunted. 'Come in the house and wash your hands.'

In the kitchen as I bent over the brown earthenware sink I kept glancing across at the oven.

Mrs Butler laughed. 'Oh he's still with us. Come and have a look.'

It was difficult to see the kitten in the dark interior but when I spotted him I put out my hand and touched him and he turned his head towards me.

'Doesn't often fail.' The farmer's wife lifted him out. 'I think he's a little tough 'un.' She began to spoon warm milk into the tiny mouth. 'I reckon we'll have him lappin' in a day or two.'

'You're going to keep him, then?'

'Too true we are. I'm going to call him Moses.'

'Moses?'

'Aye, you found him among the rushes, didn't you?'

I laughed. 'That's right. It's a good name.'

I was on the Butler farm about a fortnight later for the ever recurring job of 'cleansing' a cow and I kept looking around for Moses.

Farm cats have a pretty good time. They may not be petted or cosseted but it has always seemed to me that they lead a free, natural life. They are expected to catch mice but if they are not so inclined there is abundant food at hand; bowls of milk here and there and the dogs' dishes to be raided if anything interesting is left over. I had seen plenty of cats around today, some flitting nervously away, others friendly and purring. There was a tabby loping gracefully across the cobbles and a big tortoiseshell was curled on a bed of straw at the warm end of the byre;

cats are connoisseurs of comfort. But there was no sign of Moses.

I finished drying my arms and was about to make a casual reference to the kitten when Mr Butler handed me my jacket. 'Come round here with me if you've got a minute,' he said. 'I've got summat to show you.'

I followed him through the door at the end and across a passage into the long, low-roofed piggery. He stopped at a pen about half way down and pointed inside.

'Look 'ere,' he said.

I leaned over the wall and my face must have shown my astonishment because the farmer burst into a shout of laughter.

'That's summat new for you, isn't it?'

I stared unbelievingly down at a large sow stretched comfortably on her side, suckling a litter of about twelve piglets and right in the middle of the long pink row, furry black and incongruous, was Moses. He had a teat in his mouth and was absorbing his nourishment with the same rapt enjoyment as his smooth-skinned fellows on either side.

'What the devil . . .?' I gasped.

Mr Butler was still laughing. 'I thought you'd never have seen anything like that before, I never have, any road.'

'But how did it happen?' I still couldn't drag my eyes away.

'It was the Missus's idea,' he replied. 'When she'd got the little

youth lappin' milk she took him out to find a right warm spot for him in the buildings. She settled on this pen because the sow, Bertha, had just had a litter and I had a heater in and it was grand and cosy.'

I nodded. 'Sounds just right.'

'Well she put Moses and a bowl of milk in here,' the farmer went on, 'but the little feller didn't stay by the heater very long – next time I looked in he was round at t'milk bar.'

I shrugged my shoulders. 'They say you see something new every day at this game, but this is something I've never even heard of.'

I never went to the Butler's without having a look in the pig pen. Bertha, his foster mother, seemed to

find nothing unusual in this hairy intruder and pushed him around casually with pleased grunts just as she did with the rest of her brood.

Moses for his part appeared to find the society of the pigs very congenial. When the piglets curled up together and settled down for a sleep Moses would be somewhere in the heap and when his young colleagues were weaned at eight weeks he showed his attachment to Bertha by spending most of his time with her.

And it stayed that way over the years. Often he would be right inside the pen, rubbing himself happily along the comforting bulk of the sow, but I remember him best in his favourite place; crouching on the wall looking down on what had been his first warm home.

Sowing and Growing

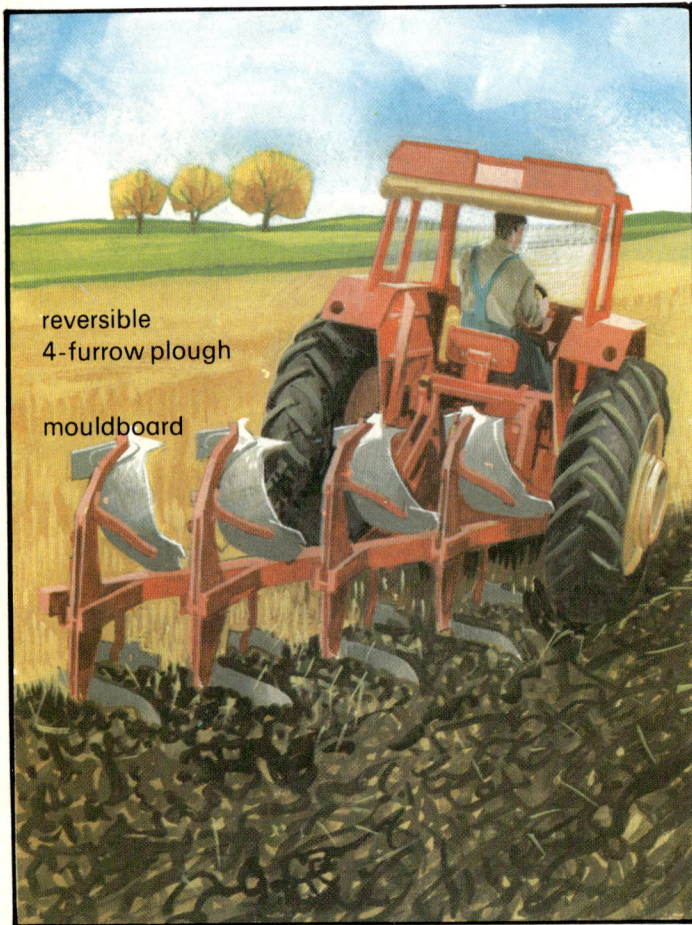

reversible
4-furrow plough

mouldboard

disc-harrow

spring-tine cultivator

Ploughing

The farming year begins in the autumn when the soil is ploughed after the harvest. Ploughing prepares the soil for the next season's crop.

The plough is pulled along by a tractor. Two sharp blades, the **coulter** and the **share,** cut a slice out of the soil leaving a deep channel or furrow. Another piece called the **mouldboard** makes the slice turn upside-down. The weeds, stubble and the insect pests that were at the surface are buried underground. If the farmer has spread manure on the field before ploughing, this is buried too.

A large plough may have four, five or even more mouldboards so that it turns over several furrows at once.

Cultivating

The winter frosts break up the earth into small lumps. Then a cultivator can be used to break it into fine crumbs. There are special cultivators for preparing seed-beds.

The **spring-tine cultivator** has rows of sharp, curved spikes mounted on springs so that they hammer at the lumps of soil as it is dragged along.

The **disc-harrow** has sharp, saucer-shaped blades which slice through the topsoil.

Farmers plant a different kind of crop in each field every year. This gives the soil a chance to recover some of the 'plant food' that the last crop took from it. This system is called 'rotating the crops'.

combine seed drill

aerial spraying

boom sprayer

Sowing

Seeds are usually planted with a machine called a **seed drill.** This has a row of sharp little wheels called coulters which cut shallow grooves in the soil. Behind each coulter is a tube. Seeds from the seed box pour down the tubes and into the grooves in the soil.

With a combine seed drill, **fertiliser** can be put down with the seeds to make the soil rich and help the seedlings to grow.

The seeds take from one to two weeks to start sprouting, depending on the temperature of the air and the soil.

Some vegetable seedlings have to be spaced out. This can be done by **transplanting** machines.

Spraying

When the crops start to grow, the weeds must be prevented from smothering the small plants. Weeds can be killed off by spraying the crops with a **selective weed-killer.** This does not harm the crops but can be dangerous to wildlife or people if used carelessly.

Crops can be sprayed with fertiliser, and chemical sprays are used to kill off insect pests. Unfortunately, many sprays also kill harmless insects, or poison birds who feed on the pests.

Crops are usually sprayed from a boom sprayer, fixed to a tractor. Large fields are sprayed from the air.

All plants need water to grow, so during a drought, or in dry places, crops have to be watered, or **irrigated.**

Seeds and Cuttings

The Pip Race

You will need

fruit pips

good soil

water

pin

yoghurt pots

saucers

1. Prick holes in the bottoms of the pots. Fill them with damp soil.

2. Push a pip gently into the soil. Cover it up. Put other pips in other pots. Label each one.

3. Water saucer to keep soil damp. The pips may take three weeks to sprout.

4. Count the days until each shoot appears. Which fruit wins? Which one grows the biggest?

The Cutting Race

You will need

pin, pencil

yoghurt pots

sharp scissors

saucers

water

good soil

healthy house plant

1. Prick holes in the bottoms of the yoghurt pots and fill them with damp soil.

2. Cut some new side-shoots off a healthy plant. Trim off extra leaves.

cut here

3. Make hole in soil with pencil. Push stalk in gently. Press soil around stalk.

4. Have a race between 3 cuttings. How many leaves does each one grow? Water them to keep the soil damp.

Grow the seedlings and cuttings on a windowsill but not in hot sunlight.

Water the saucers to keep the soil damp.

Keep a diary to show how fast they grow.

The Lonely Scarecrow

by James Kirkup

My poor old bones—I've only two—
A broomshank and a broken stave.
My ragged gloves are a disgrace.
My one peg-foot is in the grave.

I wear the labourer's old clothes:
Coat, shirt and trousers all undone.
I bear my cross upon a hill
In rain and shine, in snow and sun.

I cannot help the way I look.
My funny hat is full of hay.
—O, wild birds, come and nest in me!
Why do you always fly away?

Farm Machinery

baler

swathe-turner

mowing machine

Old hay-making tools

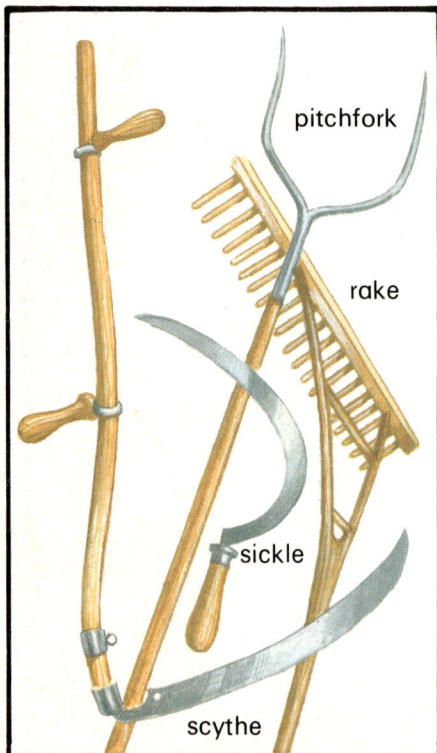

pitchfork

rake

sickle

scythe

On a modern farm, there are hundreds of tools and many large complicated machines, just as there are in a large factory.

All the tools have to be looked after carefully so that they will be ready when they are needed. Before using the tools and machines they should be checked to see that they are safe and working properly. They may have to be greased, oiled or sharpened. If a machine has an engine, like the tractor and the combine, this has to be serviced and refuelled regularly, just like a car.

A farmer is always having to mend bits of machinery. There are gates, fences and buildings to repair too. A farm mechanic is kept busy all the time as different machines are needed in each season.

At hay-making time, four of the machines shown in the picture will be needed. The **mowing machine** is attached

forage harvester

elevator

to a tractor and used to cut the grass. The wheels of the **swathe-turner** turn over the stalks so that they dry out quickly to make hay. The hay is left in long rows which are gathered up by the **baler.** It picks up the loose pieces and packs them firmly into bales and drops them out behind. The bales are built up into hay-stacks. A mechanical **elevator** is needed to carry bales up to the top layers.

Hay is used to feed livestock in winter. The animals can also be fed on **silage** which is made from leafy crops or young, green grass. The **forage harvester** cuts the grass, chops and mashes it up, and blows the mixture out of a spout into a trailer towed behind. The mixture is then pressed and stored undercover to turn it into silage for the winter.

This may seem to be a lot of machinery just for harvesting grass, but it is a very important crop.

Building a haystack the old way

Tractor and Tools

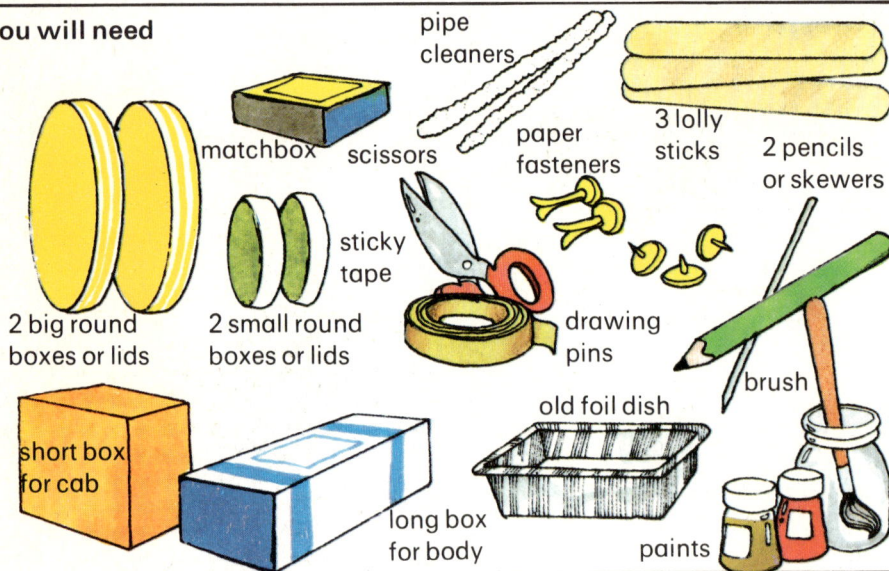

You will need

pipe cleaners

matchbox scissors

paper fasteners

3 lolly sticks

2 pencils or skewers

2 big round boxes or lids

2 small round boxes or lids

sticky tape

drawing pins

brush

short box for cab

long box for body

old foil dish

paints

1. Tape small box onto long box to make tractor body and safety cab.

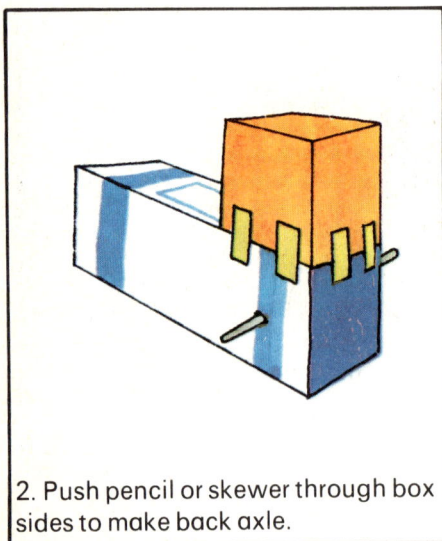

2. Push pencil or skewer through box sides to make back axle.

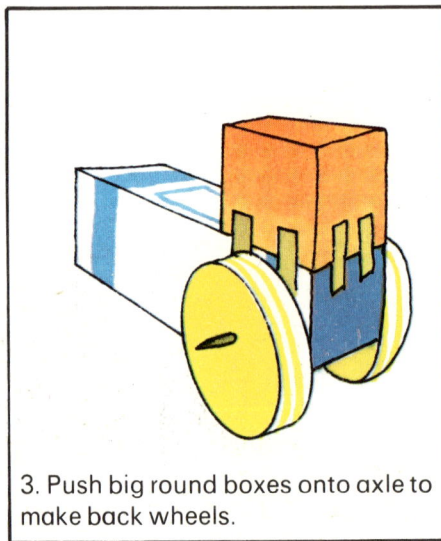

3. Push big round boxes onto axle to make back wheels.

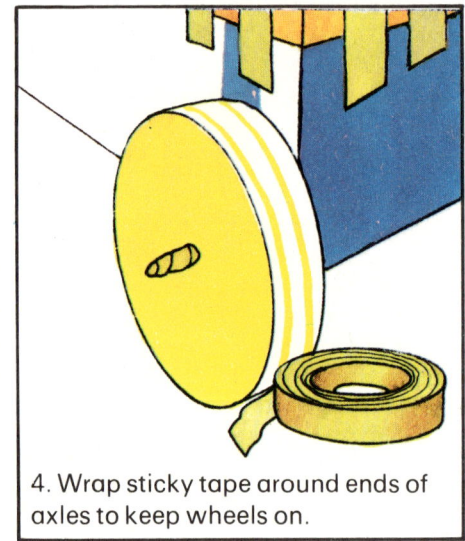

4. Wrap sticky tape around ends of axles to keep wheels on.

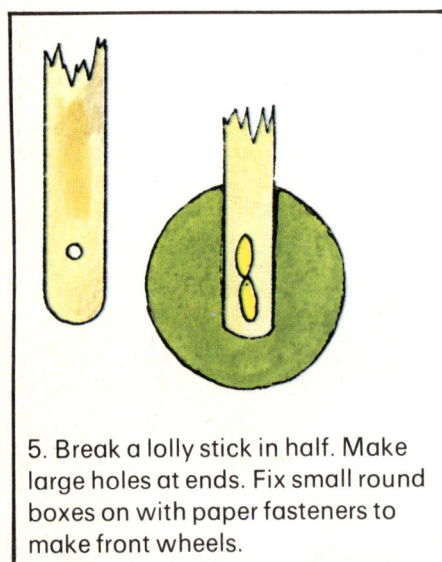

5. Break a lolly stick in half. Make large holes at ends. Fix small round boxes on with paper fasteners to make front wheels.

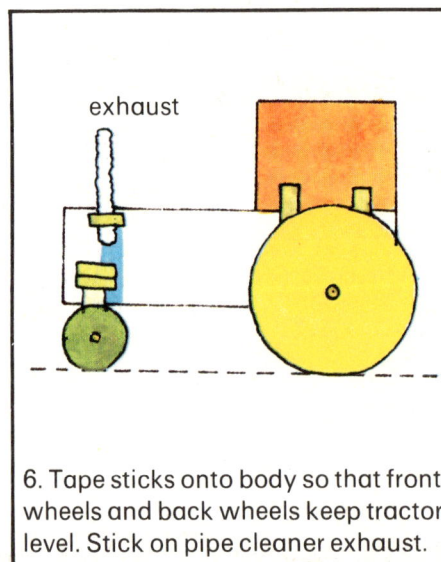

exhaust

6. Tape sticks onto body so that front wheels and back wheels keep tractor level. Stick on pipe cleaner exhaust.

7. Put paper fastener in back of tractor for attaching tools. Paint your tractor. Paint a driver in the cab.

8. Cut plough from old foil dish. Bend up blades. Fix to body with pipe cleaners.

9. Cut discs for harrow from foil. Thread discs onto pencil. Attach to tractor with pipe cleaners.

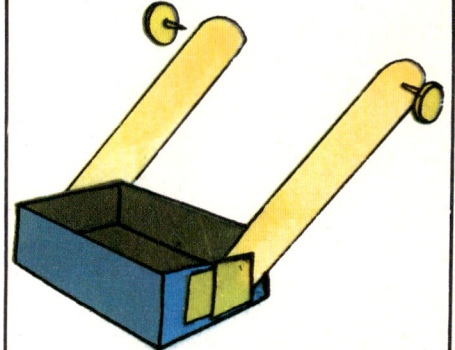

10. Make front loader by taping lolly sticks to matchbox. Fix onto tractor with drawing pins.

A tractor is the most useful machine on a farm. It can be used for pulling, pushing and carrying. How many different ways of using a tractor can you think of?

Sheep

sheep dip

Plan of the course at a sheepdog trial

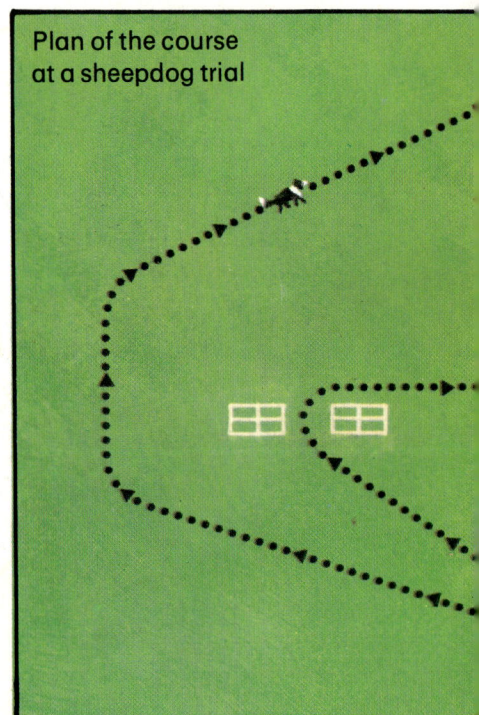

At one time, sheep were reared for the milk they gave. Nowadays, the milk is drunk by their lambs and the sheep provide us with meat and wool.

There are many different breeds. Some produce long, fine wool, others have a much shorter, wiry fleece.

The shepherd's year begins in early autumn at the time of the sheep sales. All the sheep are rounded up and inspected to see that they are healthy. Old ewes that have had several lambs may be sold off. New young ewes may be bought and added to the flock.

The ewes are mated with a ram and put out to graze on good pasture. They have to be well fed so that they will produce plenty of milk for their lambs in spring.

Lambing time is a very busy time for shepherds. They may have to help some of the ewes give birth to lambs, especially if there are twins. The shepherd has to make sure that every lamb has a mother to feed from.

shearing shed

Sometimes a ewe has triplets, or dies. Then a ewe whose lamb has died has to be persuaded to adopt an orphan lamb. The dead lamb's skin is wrapped around the orphan lamb. Then the new mother will let it feed from her.

During the summer the sheep-shearing takes place. The whole fleece is clipped off the sheep in one piece. Afterwards, all the sheep are branded or marked, and the whole flock is counted.

Later in the summer, the sheep are **dipped**. They are made to swim through a tank of disinfectant which will kill off the maggots and ticks on their skin. Some sheep are sprayed instead of being dipped.

Every time the flock has to be rounded up, the shepherd is helped by specially-trained dogs. At the shepherd's signal of a whistle or a shout, the dogs run round the sheep, making them move to the right place. A good dog can even single out one sheep from a huge flock.

Market Race

Play this game with your friends. You will need a dice, a shaker and some counters. First, take turns to throw the dice. The person who throws the highest number starts. Then each person throws in turn, and moves his counter the number of places shown on the dice. If you land on a yellow square you must do what the instructions tell you.

The first person to reach the market with their produce is the winner.

When you get to the Sale you have to choose between two different kinds of farming. Decide whether to buy cows, and become a dairy farmer, or buy a tractor and grow crops.

In this game, dairy farmers have to take a longer path, but may have more luck.

Record milk yield. Double your next throw.

New milking parlour. Move on 3 squares.

Cow calves. Have another turn

Hire lorry for cows. Move on 4 squares.

Cow sick. Go back 2 squares to 'phone vet.

Get a lift from a friend. Go straight to Sale.

Hikers leave gate open. Miss a turn to round up cows.

Put up electric fence. Move on 2 squares.

Set off for Sale. START

Bull wins prize at show. Have another turn.

Bull chases inspector. Move on 3 squares.

Bad weather delays harvest. Go back 2 squares.

Make butter and cheese. Move on 2 squares.

Friends help with harvest. Move on 3 squares.

Clean cows before selling them. Miss a turn.

Oversleep after harvest supper. Miss a turn.

Fine spell of weather. Move on 2 squares.

Take produce to market. Move on 2 squares.

Swarm of insect pests. Miss turn to spray crops.

YOU HAVE WON

Cows go left.

Win ploughing competition. Double your next throw.

Decide whether to buy cows or tractor.

Stop for a chat. Miss a turn.

SALE

Tractors go right.

Sow seed. Miss turn to build a scarecrow.

Drive tractor home. Move on 2 squares.

Run out of diesel fuel. Walk back to Sale.

Ploughshare breaks. Go back 2 squares.

Plough fields in record time. Move on 3 squares.

The Weather

Floods

Everyone who lives or works on a farm has to be prepared to go out in every kind of weather. People who live in towns usually like sunshine and hate the cold and the rain, but the farmers need all three.

Cold frosts are needed to break up the earth in winter. The cold also kills off insect pests that live in the soil. Strong winds help to dry out the soil and make it fine and crumbly. Rain is needed to make seeds sprout and young plants grow. The crops must have enough moisture to make the ears of corn swell and the root vegetables and fruit get plump. Too much moisture can make the hay and root crops become sodden and go mouldy and rotten. To stop this happening, drainpipes are laid under some fields, and ditches are cleaned out regularly. This stops the ground from becoming waterlogged or flooded.

Crops need sunshine to ripen them. When they are ready to be harvested, the farmers and their helpers

gather them all in, as quickly as possible, before the
weather changes.

Livestock reared out of doors have to be protected
from the weather, too. Farmers choose breeds that are
suitable for their farms. The hardy breeds of sheep
and cattle that live on hill farms have thick coats
and strong short legs. Lowland breeds of dairy cattle
do not need to be as tough.

Farmers have to feed their animals on hay, silage or
roots during the winter when the grass is not growing.
If the grass stops growing in a long drought, farmers
may have to buy expensive food from other countries.

When it looks as if it is going to snow, farmers
bring their animals to sheltered fields near their
farmhouses. Then food can be taken out to them easily.
Sometimes sheep are buried under snow in a sudden
blizzard. The animals usually have the sense to
huddle together in a sheltered place. Sheepdogs smell
them out and show the rescuers where to dig.

Drought

The Harvest

Farmers watch their crops carefully and hope for the right amount of sun, rain and wind to make their crops ripen safely.

As each crop ripens, it is harvested. Fortunately, different crops are ready to be harvested at different times of the year. It would be difficult for farmers if potatoes needed digging up at hay-making time, or if apples needed picking at the same time as peas.

At the end of the summer there is the grain harvest when the cereal crops are harvested. Cereals, which include wheat, barley, maize, rye, oats and rice, are some of the most important foods for people and for farm animals.

Cereals are grown in many countries. On the great plains of North America, Australia and Russia, millions of tonnes of wheat are harvested, using huge combine harvesters. These giant machines cut the crop and thresh or beat out the grain from the ears, or seed heads. The grain is blown along a pipe, collected in a tank and then poured into a truck, leaving the stalks, or straw, behind. This is pressed into bales and stacked in the farmyard. It can be used as feed for some of the animals during the winter, or for their bedding. The grain is put through a grain drier and is stored in huge bins or tower silos. Some of the grain will be used to feed animals. Wheat is sold to be ground into flour.

For thousands of years, people have held harvest festivals to celebrate the end of a good harvest because it means they will have enough food for the winter.

The six most important cereal crops

oats

rye

maize

rice

wheat

barley

The Corn Goddess

by Ralph Whitlock

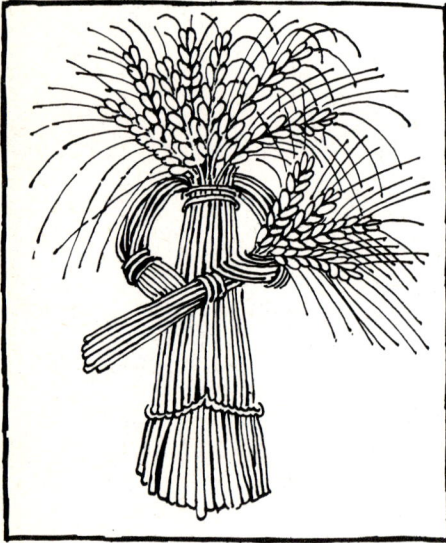

At last the wheat was ready for harvest. The men of the village had sharpened their sickles on their whetstones. Now they stood lined up along one side of the great field in which every family had its share. The women stood beside them, ready to gather the fallen stalks of corn and to tie them into sheaves. Even the children were there, eager to pick up the stray ears.

Throughout the year everyone had laboured hard in the fields – ploughing, sowing, harrowing, weeding. Now all was ready for the villagers to reap the reward for all their work. Soon the grain would be safely gathered and stored in the barns, so that no-one would starve during the coming winter.

Herman watched his father testing the sharpness of the sickle with his thumb. A breeze came fluttering over the field, bending the heads of the wheat. A skylark leapt suddenly from the corn and soared skywards, unwinding its golden chain of song.

'Look out! He's nearly ready,' said Herman's father.

He was looking at a broad, bearded man in the middle of the rank of reapers. The man's name was Thorn, and he was The Lord of the Harvest. It was he who got the men lined up, gave the signal to start, said when they were to stop to eat, and organised the work. He raised his sickle high

in the air and shouted 'Ready.' Then, when he stooped, every other man also stooped and began cutting the corn with his sickle. The harvest had begun.

Herman selected straight stalks, about six together, and handed them to his mother. She twisted them together and used them for tying the sheaves. Then he helped to stand the sheaves in bunches, so that they could dry in the sunshine.

At mid-day they sat on the hedge-bank and ate their bread-and-cheese. At tea-time the grandmothers brought out more food and drink. Work went on until sunset. Then everyone went home, very tired.

The harvest lasted for more than a month. At last only a narrow strip remained of all the corn which had been growing in the great field. Thorn straightened his back. He stood upright and looked around. Everyone stopped work. Thorn took off his hat and laid it on the ground.

'Here she is!' he exclaimed.

He knelt on one knee and very gently cut the last stalks of corn.

A great shout went up from all the harvesters.

'Hurrah! Hurrah! We've done it!' they yelled.

They tossed their hats in the air

and threw their arms around each other.

Thorn's wife gathered up the last precious stalks and gave them to him.

He went and sat under a big oak tree in a corner of the field. Herman crept up behind him and watched him. Thorn was weaving the stalks into a pattern.

'Come out from behind that tree-trunk,' said Thorn, without looking up. Herman walked around slowly and stood in front of Thorn. He had thought the man had not seen him.

'Do you know what this is?' demanded Thorn.

'No,' said Herman.

'It's the Corn Goddess,' Thorn told him. 'There! Do you think it begins to look anything like a lady?'

He had woven the stalks into the shape of a lady with a long skirt. There were ears of wheat for her hair and her hands. Now he was weaving a little straw basket to be carried on her arm.

'All the year we all work hard in the fields,' he said. 'We plough the good earth. We sow the seed. We watch it grow and keep it free from weeds. We chase away the crows, the pigeons and the sparrows. We prevent the farm animals from straying into the fields. But when we have done all this, we have done only about half of what is

needed. The wheat must have sunlight and rain. There must be frost to crumble the soil. Above all, there must be life in the seed.'

'All this is a great mystery. We can do nothing about it. We have to trust in the Corn Goddess, who lives in the soil. It is she who causes the wheat to grow and who gives us a harvest. She lives in the harvest.'

'As the reapers work, moving across the field, so she is left with less and less corn for her home. At last there is only one small strip of standing corn left. That is why I cut it so carefully. She was in those last stalks of corn.'

'I am weaving those stalks into the shape of a goddess, so that everyone can see her and thank her for our harvest.'

Herman was very interested. So Thorn showed him how to twist and weave the stalks into patterns.

'One day, when I am too old, perhaps you will have the honour of fashioning the Corn Goddess at harvest time,' he said. But he would not let Herman touch the image of the Corn Goddess that he had made.

'She must be treated with great care and respect,' he warned. 'If we were to offend her, she might not give us a good harvest next year. Then we would starve.'

When all the sheaves were dry they were taken back to the village to be stored in the great barn. The people formed a procession and marched to the barn, singing and shouting. At their head marched Thorn, the Lord of the Harvest, carrying the straw Corn Goddess.

That evening they had a Harvest Feast. They had newly-baked bread from the wheat they had harvested; butter and cheese from the cows on the village pastures; beef from a roasted ox; vegetables from the village gardens; ale brewed from the barley they had grown in their fields; sweetmeats made from apples and blackberries and other fruits of the orchards and hedgerows. They made speeches. They sang old Harvest songs. They drank toasts. And there, perched on a barrel at the head of the table, sat the Corn Goddess. They placed a loaf of bread and a glass of ale by her side, to show how grateful they were.

When it was all over, Thorn took her back to his house, where she was given a place of honour on the mantelshelf over the hearth. There she remained till after the Feast of Yule, which we call Christmas. Then, when the days began to lengthen again the villagers held the Feast of the Plough. They decorated their ploughs and had another splendid feast. Then they marched to the fields to start work for the next harvest.

When Thorn had ploughed the first furrow, he took the straw Corn Goddess which he had made and laid her gently in it. All the people knelt and prayed, asking her to give them another good harvest. Then Thorn ploughed another furrow, turning the dark brown soil over the Goddess and burying her. She was back in the good earth, where she belonged. Once again she could do her mysterious work that caused the seed to grow.

Herman, Thorn and their families lived long, long ago. But people have remembered the art of straw weaving. The figures made are called Corn Dollies, or Kern Babies.

Corn Dollies

You will need
drinking straws
rod
elastic bands
scissors
pencil

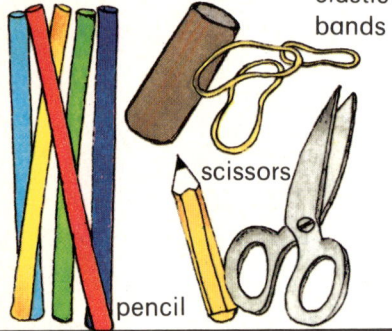

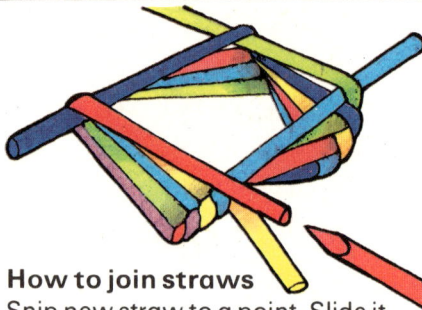

How to join straws
Snip new straw to a point. Slide it into the old one. Avoid joins where straws bend.

How to finish off
Tuck last straw under one below at a corner. Snip off long ends.

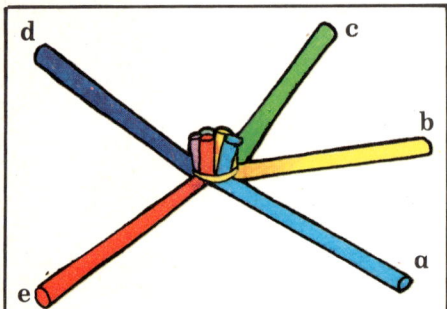

1. Tie five different coloured straws together with elastic band. Fan out long ends on table. Call them **a**, **b**, **c**, **d** and **e**.

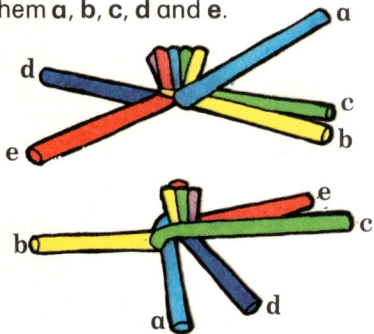

2. Bend each straw in turn over the next two straws to the right. That is, bend **a** over **b** and **c**, then **c** over **a** and **d**, then **d** over **c** and **e**, and so on.

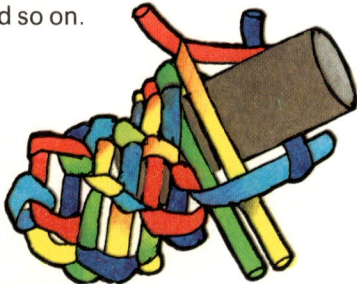

3. Continue making spiral upwards. Use pencil, rod or tube in centre to make shape wider or narrower.

Spiral weaving

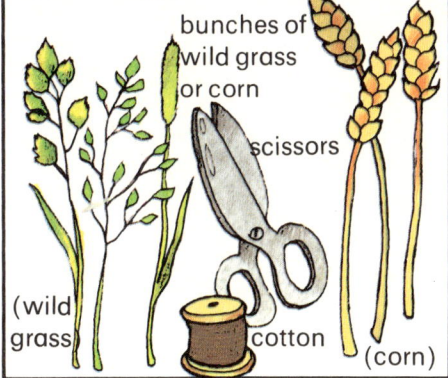

You will need

bunches of wild grass or corn

scissors

(wild grass

cotton

(corn)

1. Choose large bunch of grass or corn for doll. Arrange ears to make head. Save small pieces.

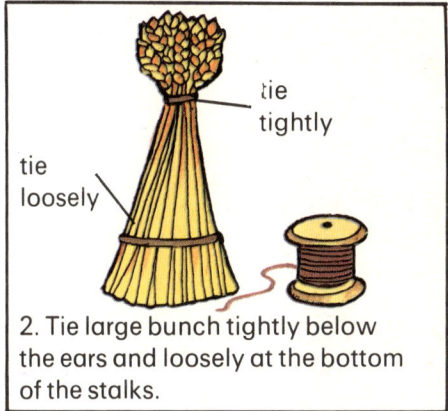

tie tightly

tie loosely

2. Tie large bunch tightly below the ears and loosely at the bottom of the stalks.

Straw Maiden

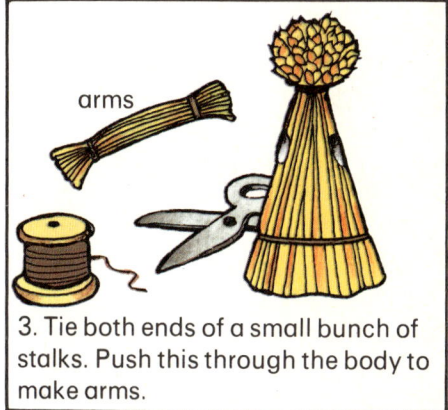

arms

3. Tie both ends of a small bunch of stalks. Push this through the body to make arms.

sheaf

4. Bend arms round. Tie waist below arms. Tie small bunch of ears to make sheaf.

stuffing

5. Put sheaf in arms. Stuff skirt with odd ends of stalks to make doll stand firmly.

apples

pears

damsons

cherries

hazelnuts

walnuts

oranges

chestnuts

lemons

almonds

peaches

strawberries

36

Fruit and Nuts

Two kinds of crops which do not have to be planted every year are fruit and nuts. These trees and bushes come into flower each spring. Insects carry pollen from flower to flower which makes the tiny seed at the heart of each flower begin to grow. During blossom-time, cold frosts and birds are the great danger as both can damage the fruit before it is properly formed. When the fruit starts to swell, insects are the enemy. Then the trees are sprayed with **insecticide** which kills the grubs and **fungicide** which prevents fungus damaging the leaves.

The trees have to be cared for in other ways too. Once a year, some of them have to be **pruned** by cutting back some of the shoots. Old or diseased trees and branches have to be cut down. New trees have to be planted and protected.

When the fruit is ripe, hundreds of people are needed to help with the picking and packing. Soft fruits, such as peaches, are easily damaged, but some hard fruits, such as apples and nuts, are collected by machine. Tree-shakers are used to make the fruit or nuts drop off the trees. Stripping machines pull all the fruit and leaves off currant bushes. Grapes have to be cut down very carefully, even if they are going to be crushed afterwards to make wine. In wine-producing areas the grape harvest is followed by a very merry festival.

Fresh and dried fruits are exported by growers in sunny countries to customers all round the world. When you next eat some fruit, look and see whether its packaging tells you where it has come from.

Fruit from around the world

plums

melons

grapefruit

redcurrants

pomegranates

Picking grapes in a vineyard for making into wine

A Farmer's Life

Let the Wealthy and Great,
Roll in Splendour and State,
I envy them not, I declare it;
I eat my own Lamb,
My Chickens and Ham,
I shear my own Fleece and I wear it.

I have Lawns, I have Bowers,
I have Fruits, I have Flowers,
The Lark is my morning alarmer;
    So Jolly Boys now,
Here's God speed the Plough,
    Long Life and Success to the Farmer!

Jumbled Names

What a muddle! Old Farmer Giles has got all his sacks mixed up and he doesn't know which is which.

He remembers that he bought six different kinds of seed for growing cereal crops. Can you sort out the jumbled letters on each sack and find out the names of the six cereal crops?

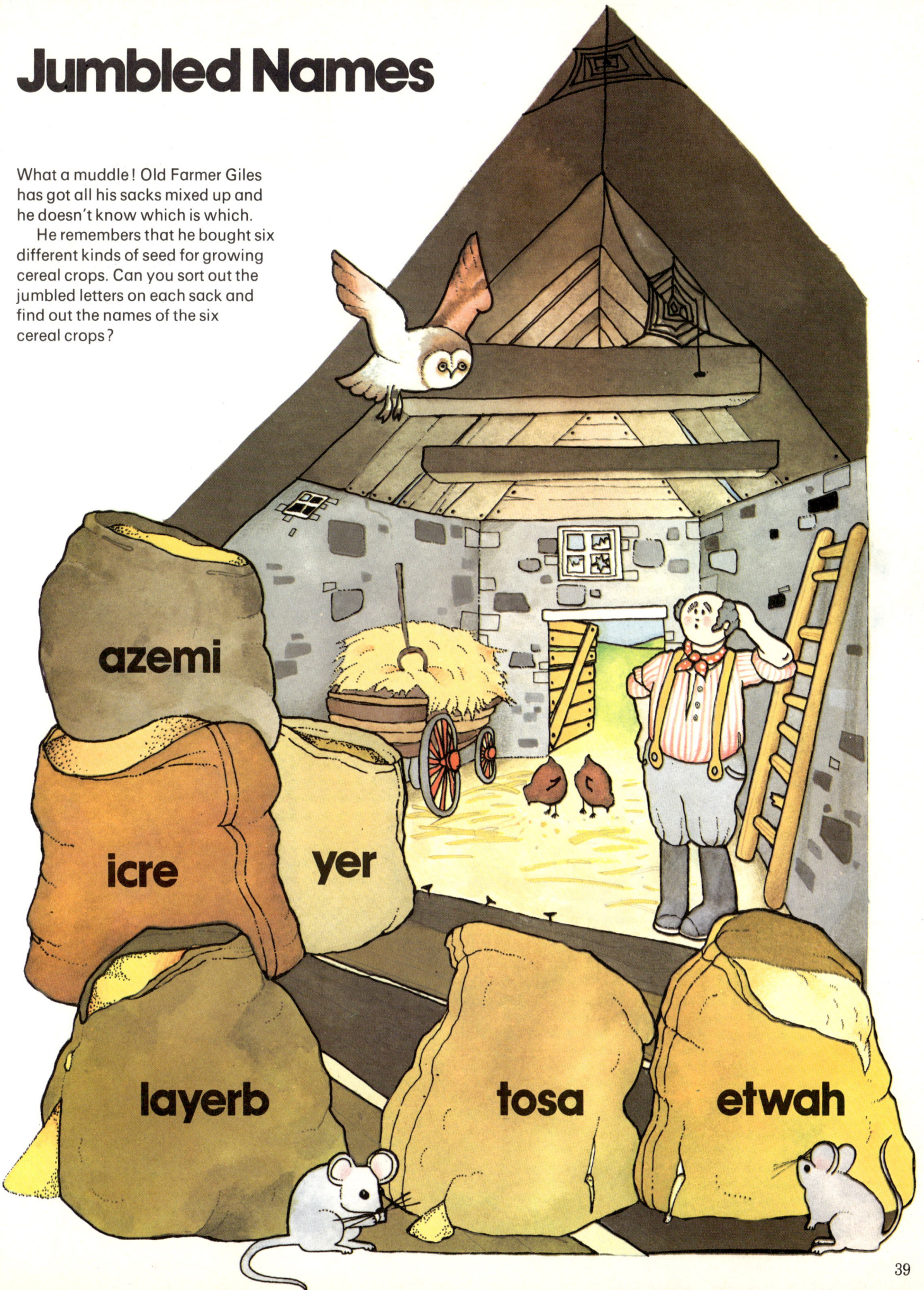

azemi

icre

yer

layerb

tosa

etwah

Poultry

incubator

brooder

rearing house

turkey

duck

Turkeys and ducks can be reared in large numbers in broiler houses, or kept outdoors.

Most chickens never see their mothers at all. Instead of leaving the hen to sit on her own eggs to hatch them out, the eggs are put into **incubators.** These look rather like bakers' ovens. They contain rows of drawers full of eggs. The eggs are kept at the right temperature for three weeks until the chicks hatch out. When the chicks are a day old they are sorted into males and females, packed into boxes and sent off to **rearing houses.**

At first, the tiny chicks need to be kept warm because they have no mother hen to nestle under. Instead, they crowd together under large, low heaters called **brooders.** The floor of the rearing house is covered with **deep-litter** which is usually made from sawdust or wood shavings. The temperature, ventilation, lighting, food and water supplies can be controlled automatically.

Some breeds of chicken lay a great many eggs, other breeds are good for fattening up quickly. When they are about six months old the egg-layers should be ready to

Battery house

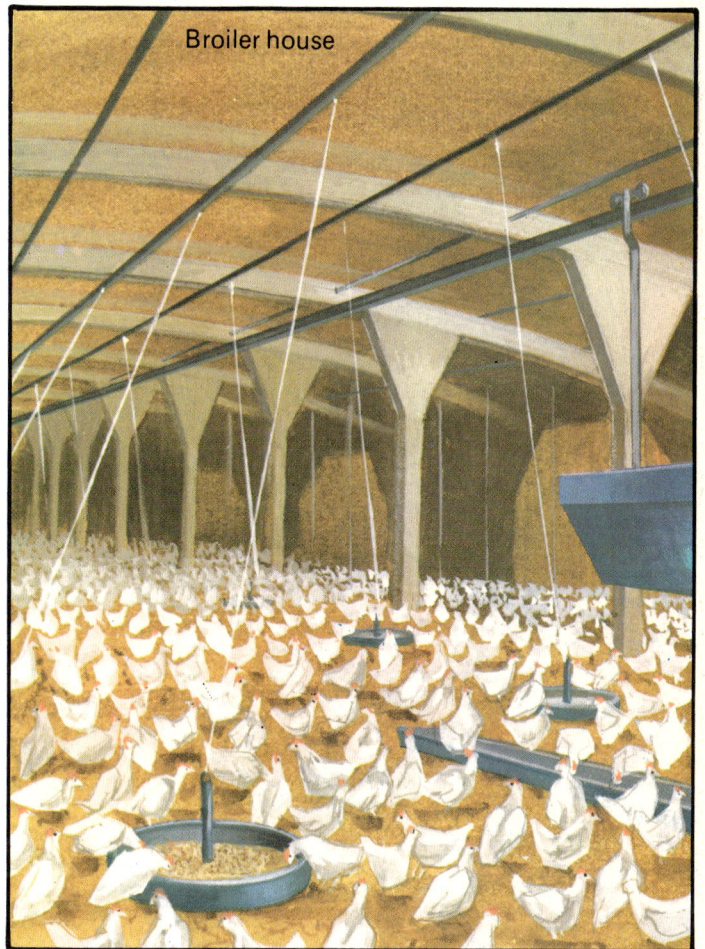
Broiler house

begin to lay and they are moved to **battery houses.**

In battery houses, the hens live in rows of wire cages. A conveyor belt brings food to the hens, another belt carries away the droppings. The cages have sloping floors so that the eggs roll out. The hens are unable to move about naturally. Some people think that this is a very cruel way to treat them.

Farmers also control the amount of light in battery houses. Normally, hens only lay eggs in the spring and summer, when the days are long and light. With bright electric lights, farmers can make hens lay all year round, so they can have eggs to sell whenever they want.

The table birds are fattened up in **broiler houses** which are very like rearing houses. They have deep-litter on the floor and automatic machinery to give the birds everything they need. As many as 10,000 birds can be reared together. Broiler chickens are slaughtered after about three months.

guinea-fowl

goose

Geese and guinea-fowl are two kinds of poultry that can only be reared outdoors on **free-range**.

At the Old Farmhouse

Cider press

Nowadays, enormous amounts of food are prepared and packed in food factories. Peas that were growing in the fields in the morning can be deep-frozen by the afternoon. Food has to be stored in a way that will **preserve** it and keep it from going bad. Deep-freezing, canning and freeze-drying are three ways of doing this.

Preserving food used to be the job of the farmer's wife and daughters. Even the smallest children would help to shell peas and prepare fruit.

Some fruit would be boiled with sugar to make jam. Fruit or vegetables were boiled in sealed bottles. Vegetables were also stored in salt or pickled in vinegar. Herbs were dried and ground up finely using a pestle and mortar.

When a big pig was slaughtered, some of the meat was rubbed with salt and hung near the fire for weeks to turn it into smoked bacon. Some meat tastes better if it is hung up for a week or more before it is eaten. Some of it may begin to smell very strongly.

Birds have to be **plucked** and **dressed** after they have

Preserving fruit

Plucking a goose

been hung. Plucking out all the feathers is quite hard work. A dressed bird is one that has had all the un-eatable parts taken out from inside it.

Almost every farm used to have its own dairy where the milk was cooled and butter and cheese were made. The cream was stirred around in a wooden **churn** until it separated into yellow lumps of butter and a milky liquid called skim milk. This was poured off and the butter was washed and patted into large blocks. Cheese was made from soured milk. When this was heated it separated into a fatty **curd** and milky liquid called **whey.** The curd was chopped up and salted and left to set hard and become cheese. It was wrapped in cloth and pressed under a large weight, or in a screw press.

Screw-presses were also used to press the juice out of apples to make cider.

Old farmhouse kitchens had just as many gadgets and machines as a modern one, but nowadays most of the machines are driven by electricity instead of being worked by hand.

Old kitchen tools

colander
ladle
pestle
mortar
butter shapers
cauldron
skimmer

Churning butter

Pressing cheese

Animal Cheese Biscuits

You will need

mixing bowl
rolling pin
baking tray
100 grammes of flour
grater
tracing paper
thin card
knife
tablespoon
water
50 grammes of cheese
50 grammes of margarine
scissors
pencil

1. Cut some animal shapes from card. (You could trace the ones on page 7).

2. Turn on the oven to 400°F (200°C) or Gas Mark 6. Put the flour into the mixing bowl.

3. Rub the margarine into the flour with your fingertips.

4. Grate the cheese and add it.

5. Add 3 tablespoons of water. Mix the pastry with a knife. Press it into a ball.

6. Roll out the pastry on a floured surface until it is half a centimetre thick.

7. Put the card animal shapes on the pastry. Cut round them with a knife.

8. Put the pastry animals on a baking tray. Bake them for 10-15 minutes.

9. Ask a grown-up to help you take them out of the oven when they are light brown.

Home-made Butter

You will need butter dish spoon screw-top jar jug of water basin bottle of milk fine sieve

1. Pour the top-of-the-milk into the jar. Put the rest of the milk back in the fridge.

2. Screw the lid on and shake the jar until little yellow specks of butter appear. (Get a friend to help).

3. Keep shaking it until the butter goes into lumps.

4. Pour off the liquid through a fine sieve. Rinse the butter with water.

5. Spoon the butter into a dish. Pat it into one lump.

Serve the animal cheese biscuits on a plate when they are cool. You could spread some of them with the home-made butter and leave some of them plain.

Hidden Pests

Farms have all sorts of pests!
Foxes try to steal chickens, pigeons
eat seeds, rabbits eat young plant
shoots. Caterpillars eat leaves and
colorado beetles like potato leaves
especially. Under the ground, moles
dig tunnels and wireworms bore into
potatoes. There are many more insect
pests.

Even people can be a menace if they
leave gates open and drop litter.

Can you find eight different kinds
of pests (or traces of them) hiding
in this picture?